Din
at the Dentist

(and other silly things)

written & illustrated

by

Jason L. Witter

Dinosaurs at the Dentist (and other silly things)

ISBN-13: 978-1981701209
ISBN-10: 1981701206

First Edition: January 2018

witterworks1@gmail.com
www.facebook.com/witterworks
Instagram: @tiniest_vampire
www.etsy.com/shop/WitterWorks

This silly book belongs to:

_____

Gigantic Thank You to my parents
LEONARD & JANE WITTER
for supporting me
every step of the way!

Executive Producers

Craig A. Butler

Maggie S

Ryan Denmark

Producers

Otis Caruth

Alison Jackson

Greg'o

Andrew Kottke

Matthew Urbaniak

and

Charlotte Urbaniak

CONTENTS

CHAPTER 1

Dinosaurs, Robots, Monsters & Tooth Brushes

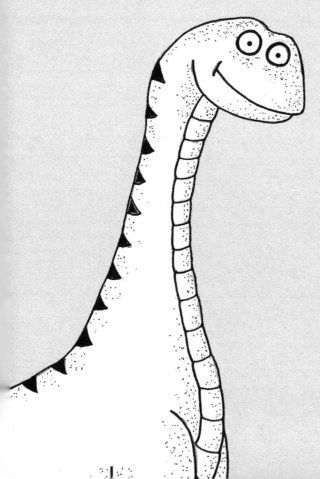

Fossil Fillings

The other dinosaurs in town
think Tyson T. Rex is a big ol' menace,
but they don't know deep down,
he just wants to be a dino-dentist!

Apple Inquiry

Robot found a worm inside an apple

and thought it could not be.

This made Robot wonder...

"Is there life inside of me?"

Having any kind of answer,

the worm could not pretend.

But it didn't really matter,

'cause they became the best of friends.

Monster Jam

Ziggy Small
is
very,
very,
very,
very,
very,
very,
very,
very,
very,
very,
very
tall.
Nothing
more
to say.
That's all.

(well, sometimes he likes to play basketball)

15.

Pangea's Got Talent

Stegosaurus Stan,
the greatest of roofed lizards,
eating only plants,
and hoping for no blizzards!
Brain no bigger
than a walnut,
spiked tail, pretty great,
but Jurassic mouths
would all shut,
when he balanced
5 plates upon his plate!

Snack Time

Look at that cute little lump!
Sitting so nice
with his big belly bump!
How in the world
did he get so adorably plump?
Well...
Remember those kids
that hung out by the mall?
Riding skateboards,
shouting & playing baseball?
One was short,
one was tall,
one smelled of cheese,
one was named Paul?
Yeah.
He ate them all.

...

Oh.

Burp.

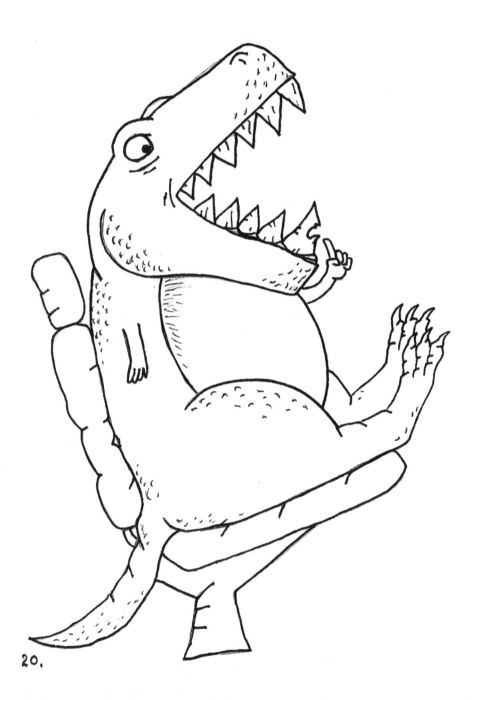

20.

Cretaceous Cavity Conundrum

Tommy T. Rex had an awful hurt.
In his tooth, there was a hole.
But no dentist would go near't,
not even with a ten foot pole!

Maybe if we found an eleven foot pole...

Caution: Sharp Edges

This demon named Denny's
been savin' his pennies,
but he hasn't got much,
'cause every time

he scrubs

his teeth,

he has

to buy

a new

tooth

brush!

That's twice a day,
I'll have you know.

I Ate What???

When Potato Monster
went to brush his teeth,
a thought hit him
just like a punch.
He had eaten
hash browns
for breakfast,
and chile
cheese fries
for lunch!

TEETH

Nose Ring

Sweet!
Robby found a basketball!
Now he's ready
to shoot,
hook & scoop!
Good thing his buddy's got it all,
including
a highly functional,
titanium,
programmable
proboscis hoop!
Swoosh!

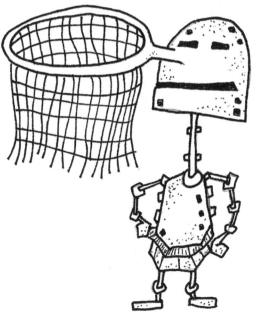

26.

Oh, Golly Lolly

I got stripes on my shirt
and circles on my lollipop.
I could not ask for more!
So, why am I not jollypop?
Well, I got a funny feeling,
it's something close to dread,
that there's a creepy creature
looming back behind my head.
What's that you say?
It's truth and not follypop?
The creepy creature's creepin' closer?
Ohhhhhhh... golly molly wollypop.

Can I at least
finish my lollipop?

Ouch

Hello, my name is Drew.

My favorite thing to do

is sit down and just kick back.

Unfortunately today,

I feel I need to say,

I think I sat on a thumb tack!

A Good Egg

Drac and Frank saw an egg
resting in their yard.
They didn't know what to do,
though they thought quite hard.
After careful evaluation
over cups of Earl Grey,
they wrapped it in a blanket
and brought it in to stay.
Then one day in June,
after going to the store,
Drac and Frank came home
to find...

... A BABY DINOSAUR!

Now Drac and Frank
have a pet Tyrannosaurus.
Two more cups of Earl Grey...
& they decided to call her Doris.
She's pretty much the best,
they think that by next year,
she'll be old enough
to join them at the Monster Fair!

(She's growing by the minute,
and it's really no big surprise
she's already expressed an interest
in funnel cake and fries.)

[SYSTEM_ERROR]

[Oh_for_goodness'_sake_

this_robot_is_eating_a_cupcake.

If_he_continues_this_tranfer_

a_malfunction_will_occur.

At_least_that_is_my suspicion_

because_though_he_is_up_to_date_

with_the_latest_data_rate_

he_has_no_digestive_system!]

CHAPTER 2

Whimsical Words, Well-Groomed Werewolves, & The Windy Ways of Change

Sharing is Scaring

Werewolf Willy & Zombie Ziddle
have an answer to life's riddle.
When they find something to eat,
they both enjoy the treat
by splitting it down the middle.

Changes

Cameron the chameleon
that crazy octogenarian...
He's lived a good while
and has no regrets.
He visited the British Isle
and paid off his debts.
He spent a bit of time
as a pirate who plundered.
He once took third place
in the Indy Five Hundred.
He's lived in Hong Kong.
He's been to Montana.
He once travelled Brazil
in a crate full of bananas.
He flew to the moon,
said it was okay,
a nice place to visit,
but he wouldn't want to stay.
His life is now mellow,
no changing colors or tricks,
he plays checkers all day...

...and watches MacGyver at six.

That young fella
sure can build
some things.

39.

Six of one,
Half Dozen of None

Sally had six arms,
and this was quite a perk.
They came in very handy
when doing her homework.
She could solve equations,
figure out X squared,
write about ol' George
crossing the Delaware.
She could do that essay
about that kid Tom Sawyer,
and jot down all her plans
to become a courtroom lawyer.
She could start a study
of spoons and like utensils,
sketch some spider monkeys
with their tails so prehensile!
She'd compose novels and create
perfect letters with her stencils.
Sally could do all this at once...
if she could only find
six pencils!

Tee-hee...

Out of Line

Tired of saying
"Arrr..."
this pirate tried
something new.
He picked
the previous letter,
and now
he's saying...

42.

Poem #18

Shall I compare thee
to a summer's day?

No?

Well, I didn't want to
anyway.

This poem upside down.

You might just be reading

And the world's turned around,

When stranger things are seeming

Which Way?

Way to Go

This Way and That Way,
those creatures with advice.
They'll tell you just how
to go and live your life.
One points over there
and offers this suggestion.
The other disagrees,
says follow that direction.
Listen to their words
and what they have to say,
but when all is said and done,
go ahead and choose
your own way!

Not Just Blowing Hot Air

You might be
completely
unaware.

But somebody,
somewhere...

Thinks you're
awesome.

So, there.

The Wolf Man's Final Big Night

The Wolf Man had yet another date,

so he wanted to look great.

But when he donned a vest & tie...

He looked awesome! I ain't gonna lie.

Drawn to Greatness

I have the motivation
to be an awesome illustration.
Everyone's eyes
I will certainly catch.
But I curb my anticipation,
content with the realization
that I am currently
just a quick sketch.

Sock It to Me

Once upon a time,

there was a writer without a rhyme.

No matter how he tried,

he just could not find

the right words that tied

the ideas in his mind.

He looked high on a shelf.

He looked under some stones.

He looked inside himself,

but there were only bones.

After searching many days,

well, maybe three or four,

he found some tucked away

inside his old sock drawer.

But these were not the best

nouns, adjectives or verbs;

he hopes he can find the rest

'cause now he's out of words...

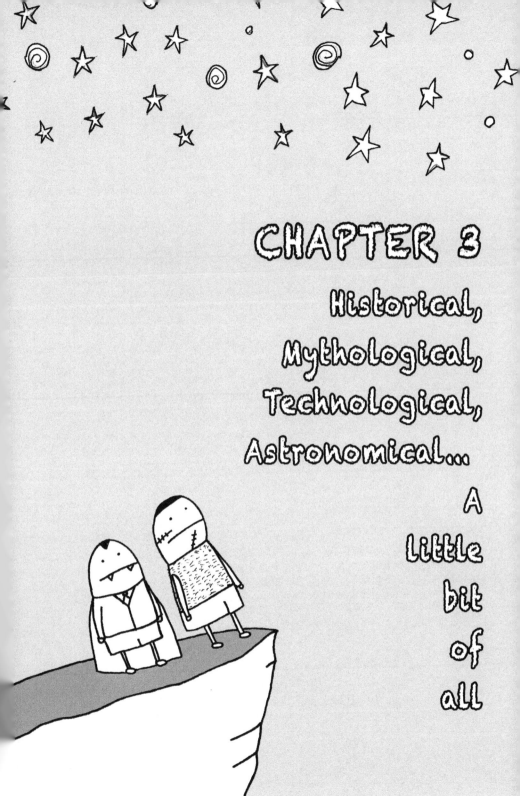

CHAPTER 3

Historical, Mythological, Technological, Astronomical...

A little bit of all

Cyclollipops

Silent candy shops...
Cyclops buys two lollipops,
Crunch! Silence now stops.

Vincent van Gogh
(a biography)

Vincent van Gogh
had a brother named Theo.
Vincent van Gogh
did not play in a jazz trio.
Vincent van Gogh
sold one picture in his life.
Vincent van Gogh
never married a wife.
Vincent van Gogh
is sometimes called quaint.
Vincent van Gogh
decided to eat yellow paint.
Vincent van Gogh
starry nights and sunflowers.
Vincent van Gogh
possibly took a few showers.
Vincent van Gogh
was not born in Delaware.
Vincent van Gogh
went and cut off his ear.

Timeless

In the land before time,

there were no clocks to chime,

telling you when you were late.

So, cavemen never were on time

(in the land before time)

when picking up their dates.

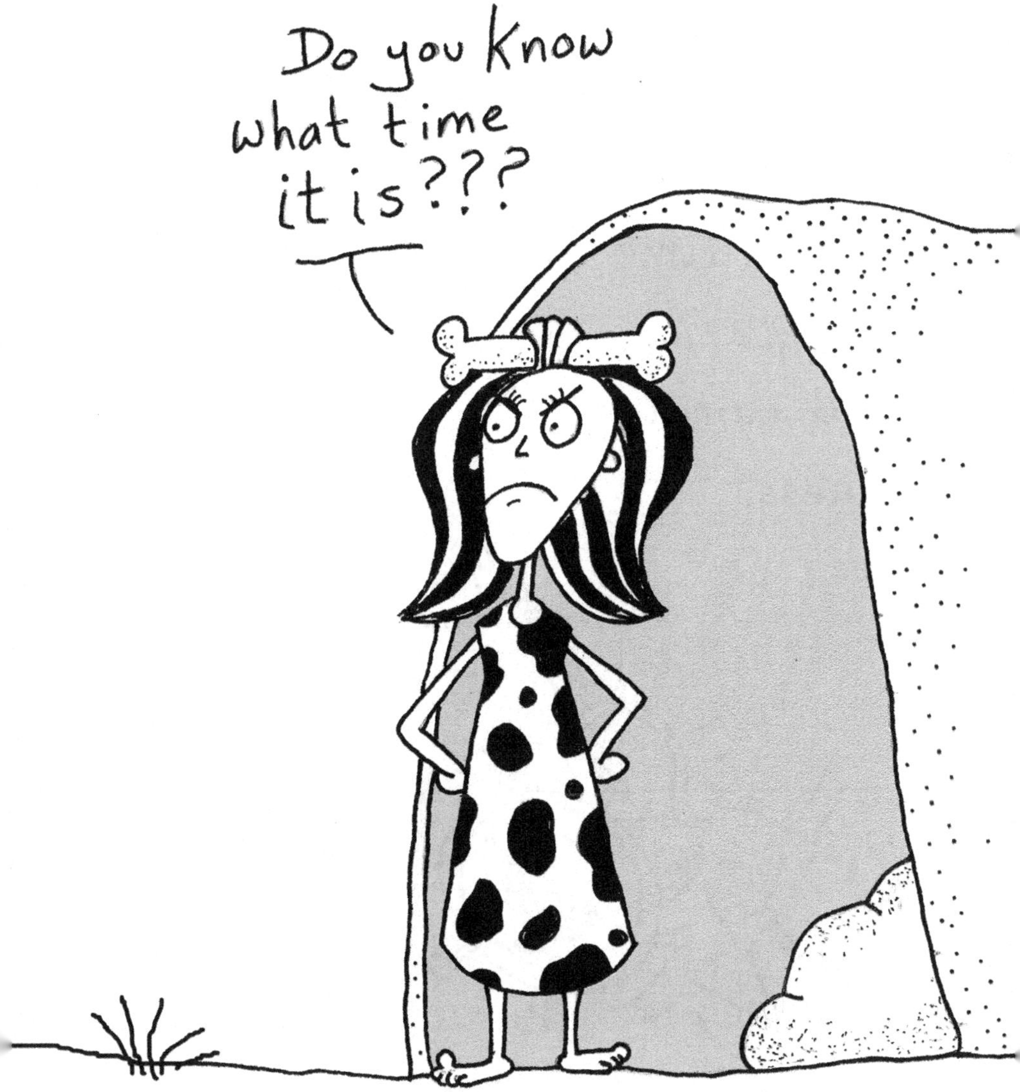
Do you know
what time
it is???

Ode to an Alarm Clock

Huh? Whazzat?
What's happening??
Some kind of warning???
Turmoil, trouble, unrest????
Oh.
It's just time to get up.
Well, fine...
good morning.
I guess.

Nature of Operation.	Variables acted upon.	Variables receiving results.	Indication of change in the value on any Variable.	Statement of Results.	Data.			
					$^1V_1$ $\bigcirc$ 0 0 1 $\boxed{1}$	$^1V_2$ $\bigcirc$ 0 0 2 $\boxed{2}$	$^1V_3$ $\bigcirc$ 0 0 4 $\boxed{n}$	$^0V_4$ $\bigcirc$ 0 0 0 $\boxed{}$
×	$^1V_2 \times ^1V_3$	$^1V_4, ^1V_5, ^1V_6$	$\begin{cases}^1V_2 = ^1V_2 \\ ^1V_3 = ^1V_3\end{cases}$	$= 2n$	...	2	n	$2n$
−	$^1V_4 - ^1V_1$	$^2V_4$	$\begin{cases}^1V_4 = ^2V_4 \\ ^1V_1 = ^1V_1\end{cases}$	$= 2n-1$	1	...	...	$2n-$
+	$^1V_5 + ^1V_1$	$^2V_5$	$\begin{cases}^1V_5 = ^2V_5 \\ ^1V_1 = ^1V_1\end{cases}$	$= 2n+1$	1	...	...	...
÷	$^2V_5 \div ^2V_4$	$^1V_{11}$	$\begin{cases}^2V_5 = ^0V_5 \\ ^2V_4 = ^0V_4\end{cases}$	$= \dfrac{2n-1}{2n+1}$	...	...	...	0
÷	$^1V_{11} \div ^1V_2$	$^2V_{11}$	$\begin{cases}^1V_{11} = ^2V_{11} \\ ^1V_2 = ^1V_2\end{cases}$	$= \dfrac{1}{2}\cdot\dfrac{2n-1}{2n+1}$	...	2	...	...
−	$^0V_{13} - ^2V_{11}$	$^1V_{13}$	$\begin{cases}^2V_{11} = ^0V_{11} \\ ^0V_{13} = ^1V_{13}\end{cases}$	$= -\dfrac{1}{2}\cdot\dfrac{2n-1}{2n+1} = A_0$	...	...	...	...
−	$^1V_3 - ^1V_1$	$^1V_{10}$	$\begin{cases}^1V_3 = ^1V_3 \\ ^1V_1 = ^1V_1\end{cases}$	$= n-1(=3)$	1	...	n	...
+	$^1V_2 + ^0V_7$	$^1V_7$	$\begin{cases}^1V_2 = ^1V_2 \\ ^0V_7 = ^1V_7\end{cases}$	$= 2+0 = 2$	...	2	...	...
÷	$^1V_6 \div ^1V_7$	$^3V_{11}$	$\begin{cases}^1V_6 = ^1V_6 \\ ^0V_{11} = ^3V_{11}\end{cases}$	$= \dfrac{2n}{2} = A_1$	...	...	...	...
×	$^1V_{21} \times ^3V_{11}$	$^1V_{12}$	$\begin{cases}^1V_{21} = ^1V_{21} \\ ^3V_{11} = ^3V_{11}\end{cases}$	$= B_1 \cdot \dfrac{2n}{2} = B_1 A_1$	...	...	...	...
+	$^1V_{12} + ^1V_{13}$	$^2V_{13}$	$\begin{cases}^1V_{12} = ^0V_{12} \\ ^1V_{13} = ^2V_{13}\end{cases}$	$= -\dfrac{1}{2}\cdot\dfrac{2n-1}{2n+1} + B_1 \cdot \dfrac{2n}{2}$	...	...	...	...
−	$^1V_{10} - ^1V_1$	$^2V_{10}$	$\begin{cases}^1V_{10} = ^2V_{10} \\ ^1V_1 = ^1V_1\end{cases}$	$= n-2(=2)$	1	...	...	...
−	$^1V_6 - ^1V_1$	$^2V_6$	$\begin{cases}^1V_6 = ^2V_6 \\ ^1V_1 = ^1V_1\end{cases}$	$= 2n-1$	1	...	...	...
+	$^1V_1 + ^1V_7$	$^2V_7$	$\begin{cases}^1V_1 = ^1V_1 \\ ^1V_7 = ^2V_7\end{cases}$	$= 2+1 = 3$	1	...	...	...
÷	$^2V_6 \div ^2V_7$	$^1V_8$	$\begin{cases}^2V_6 = ^2V_6 \\ ^2V_7 = ^2V_7\end{cases}$	$= \dfrac{2n-1}{3}$	...	...	...	...
×	$^1V_8 \times ^3V_{11}$	$^4V_{11}$	$\begin{cases}^1V_8 = ^0V_8 \\ ^3V_{11} = ^4V_{11}\end{cases}$	$= \dfrac{2n}{2}\cdot\dfrac{2n-1}{3}$	...	...	...	...
−	$^2V_6 - ^1V_1$	$^3V_6$	$\begin{cases}^2V_6 = ^3V_6 \\ ^1V_1 = ^1V_1\end{cases}$	$= 2n-2$	1	...	...	...
+	$^1V_1 + ^2V_7$	$^3V_7$	$\begin{cases}^2V_7 = ^3V_7 \\ ^1V_1 = ^1V_1\end{cases}$	$= 3+1 = 4$	1	...	...	...
÷	$^3V_6 \div ^3V_7$	$^1V_9$	$\begin{cases}^3V_6 = ^3V_6 \\ ^3V_7 = ^3V_7\end{cases}$	$= \dfrac{2n-2}{4}$	...	...	...	...
×	$^1V_9 \times ^4V_{11}$	$^5V_{11}$	$\begin{cases}^1V_9 = ^0V_9 \\ ^4V_{11} = ^5V_{11}\end{cases}$	$= \dfrac{2n}{2}\cdot\dfrac{2n-1}{3}\cdot\dfrac{2n-2}{4} = A_3$	...	...	...	...
×	$^1V_{22} \times ^5V_{11}$	$^0V_{12}$	$\begin{cases}^1V_{22} = ^1V_{22} \\ ^0V_{12} = ^2V_{12}\end{cases}$	$= B_3 \cdot \dfrac{2n}{2}\cdot\dfrac{2n-1}{3}\cdot\dfrac{2n-2}{3} = B_3 A_3$	...	...	...	...
+	$^2V_{12} + ^2V_{13}$	$^3V_{13}$	$\begin{cases}^2V_{12} = ^0V_{12} \\ ^2V_{13} = ^3V_{13}\end{cases}$	$= A_0 + B_1 A_1 + B_3 A_3$	...	...	...	...
−	$^2V_{10} - ^1V_1$	$^3V_{10}$	$\begin{cases}^2V_{10} = ^3V_{10} \\ ^1V_1 = ^1V_1\end{cases}$	$= n-3(=1)$	1	...	...	...
+	$^4V_{13} + ^0V_{24}$	$^1V_{24}$	$\begin{cases}^4V_{13} = ^0V_{13} \\ ^0V_{24} = ^1V_{24}\end{cases}$	$= B_7$	...	...	...	..
+	$^1V_1 + ^1V_3$	$^1V_3$	$\begin{cases}^1V_1 = ^1V_1 \\ ^1V_3 = ^1V_3 \\ ^5V_6 = ^0V_6 \\ ^5V_. = ^0V_.\end{cases}$	$= n+1 = 4+1 = 5$ .... by a Variable-card. by a Variable-card	1	...	$n+1$	..

Here f

Working Variables.

| $^0V_5$ | $^0V_6$ | $^0V_7$ | $^0V_8$ | $^0V_9$ | $^0V_{10}$ | $^0V_{11}$ | $^0V_{12}$ | $^0V_{13}$ |

The Countess of Code

Once upon a time
in the antique age
of Victorian Romanticism,
a fair maiden called Ada Lovelace
spent many a day composing
computer program algorithms.

$$-\frac{1}{2}\cdot\frac{2n-1}{2n+1} =$$

$$\frac{2n}{2} = A_1$$

$$\frac{2n}{2} = A_1$$

$$B_1\cdot\frac{2n}{2} = B_1 A_1$$

$$B_1\cdot\frac{2n}{2} = B_1 A_1$$

$$\frac{-1}{+1} + B_1.$$

$2n$

$2n+1$

0

$2n$ 2

$n-2$

$2n-1$

3

$2n-1$ 3 $2n$

$2n-2$

$2n-2$

ws a repetition of Operations

0 0

Ham & Mac's Tiny Adventure

Hamlet & Macbeth
went to the Renaissance Fair,
hoping to see their friends
Othello, Julius and King Lear.
Unfortunately,
none of them were there.
But they had each other,
so, they didn't really care.
They bought some balloons,
each ate a fried pear,
then Hamlet & Macbeth
decided they'd go again
next year,
and maybe try the
Tilt-A-Whirl...
... if they dare.

The Sand is Always Warmer

The minotaur left his maze
to move to Ocean City,
hoping for sunny days
and scenery so pretty.
But it's not as splendid,
in fact, he's out of sorts
'cause no one's complimented
his brand new Bermuda shorts.

I should've stayed in Crete.

Cyclops
Flip Flops

Simon the cyclops
searched all the shoe shops,
looking for the right style.
He spent such a long while
from Sparta on to Athens,
but as it just so happens,
he started feeling squirmy,
then he ran into Hermes
who gave him some advice.
He said, "For the best price,
go see Peter Papadopoulos
at the old Acropolis,
and while you are there
buy yourself a pair
of fancy flippy flopolis."

Stars in Her Eyes

This is Captain Moona Loona
with a smile upon her face,
'cause she knows that one day soona,
she's gonna go to outer space!

(and her space cat, Twinkles,
is going, too!)

Star Struck

Drac and Frank were told
to reach up to the stars.
They climbed and they climbed
out away and so far.
Scaling the highest peak
and peering up to the sky,
the universe asked them a question,
"So, here you are... but why?"
Curiously staring
at these cosmos so raw,
it filled them with wonder,
it filled them with awe.
The answer seemed close,
if they could just look ahead,
but Drac and Frank were content,
so back home they went
and had some hot chocolate instead.

Twinkle, Shminkle

When I saw
The twinkling star
It looked so small
Away so far.
I made a wish
To keep the star
It looked so small
Away so far.
My wish came true
I have the star
It looked so small
away so far.
Now I wish
I'd never seen that star
'cause it ain't so small,
and I have no idea
where to put it.

CHAPTER 4

Inspire, Love, Smile, Repeat

Simple Math

One plus one,
we know for sure,
that it will equal two.
But I like it much better
when one plus one
equals me and you!

Stick Figure Dreams

Stick
Figure
Dreams of
One day
Being a
Tree
Figure.

Baby Steps

When Dracula's cousin Barry
became an undead dad,
he traded in his cape (so scary)
for that sweater vest he never had.

And he loves it.

It's a nice fit.

Fur Baby

Fred and Franny
have a baby
who's all
covered in fur.
So, when it gets
cold outside,
you'll never hear
her saying "brrrr!"

Hanging Out

A walk in the park,
a hike in the woods,
in line at the store
buying canned goods,
looking at art
in the big ol' museum,
eating some lunch
of fried cheese and ham,
hearing a speech
in the city town square,
pointing at things
at the holiday fair,
going to Paris
and seeing the sights,
not speaking the language
but enjoying the lights,
or simply taking a stroll
in the neighborhood block,
attempting to find
the end of the sidewalk.

All this works fine
for a baby who's glad,
to be spending time
hanging out with his dad.

Three Letters

When the littlest of monsters
was asked to write a poem
about this thing called "LOVE,"
he knew just what to show 'em.
No need for fancy phrases,
neither sonnet nor a song,
forget the hundred dollar words,
or any of those sentences that
   seem to go on
      and on
        and on
for way too long...
No, he needed just three letters,
you can keep the rest of them.
He found the meaning of the word
by simply writing "Em-Oh-Em."

Under a Leaky Roof

Under
a
leaky
roof,
the
storm
brings
us
closer
to
each
other.

Missing Pieces

If we just look around,
we might be aware
the part that we need
is right over there.

Silly Happy

You and me, climbing a tree.

That's where we belong.

Up so high, in a bubblegum sky.

That's where we belong.

Laughing too loud, on a cantaloupe cloud.

That's where we belong.

Bouncing on a breeze, over blueberry seas.

That's where we belong.

Dipping ten toes

in marshmallow meadows.

Running our hands

through salt caramel sands.

Dancing our feet

on chocolate concrete.

Sharing a dream

on the island of endless ice cream.

That's where we belong!

It seems so far
from anything anywhere.
But being together,
it's like
we found
our way there.

And that's right where we belong.

Fort Castle Base

We found some old boards,
boxes, blankets and tape,
and built us a spot
where we could escape.
Three bandanas rolled up
became our new flags,
keeping warm in the cold
with those big sleeping bags.
Boom box and cassettes,
action figures to fight,
reading comics & laughing
under a dying flashlight.
No one could enter,
until it was heard,
correctly spoken,
the secret password.
No matter its looks,
this was the best place,
there'll never be anywhere
like Fort Castle Base.

A Guy Named Shel

For all those dubbed weird,

nerd, stink butt or geek,

this dude with a beard

told us we were unique.

He gave us a tree

that we could call friend,

and showed you and me

where the sidewalk did end.

With peppermint wind

and crimson bright sun,

moon-birds that sing,

and so many good puns.

In the stories he'd tell,

we found the place of our own.

Here's a big thank you to Shel,

for giving us a page to call home.

97.

CHAPTER 5

Birds,
Sea Creatures,
Chicken Nuggets
&
An Occasional
Elephant

Now Hiring

There once was a scarecrow
by the name of Rob.
He really liked birds,
and was not very good
at his job.

Worms of Wisdom

Three little birds

are known to sing

every little thing

is gonna be all right.

Unless you're a worm,

then you might say,

today is the day

I wanna get outta sight!

Blob & Bird

That there's Blob,
and this here's Bird.
They first met
on August the third.
They've been good friends
since that occurred
and hang out once a week
to do the Sunday crossword.

(and eat some of the salt water taffy
that, for some reason, covers Blob's house).

Bird Brain

Someone once said,
"I believe I can fly."
It rang in my head,
"I believe I can touch the sky."
So, I thought
I'd give it a try,
but I can tell you for sure,
it's a big ol' fat lie!

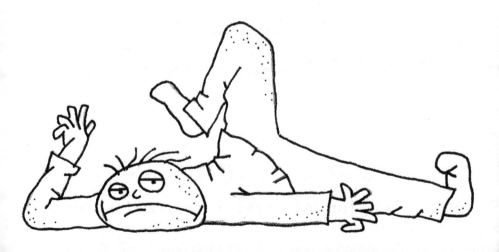

Jellyfish Wearing a Hat

Have you ever seen
a jellyfish wearing a hat?

No, I've never seen
anything like that.

Oh.
Well, here ya go.

You're welcome.

A Snail Tale

Dale is a snail.
He does not
have an e-mail.
He will never need
the latest laptop.
He will never need
to buy things via airdrop.
He will never need
to make time for speed dating.
He will never need
to worry how costs are inflating.
He will never need
the smartest cell phone.
He will never need
to take out an 8% loan

to buy that house
in the corner cul-de-sac
'cause he has a nice home
right there on his back.
He's really quite happy,
his best friend is Gale.
Life ain't too shabby
for Dale the snail.

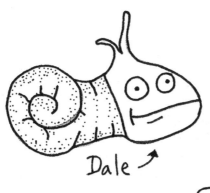

Dale →

Gale

Gale is some sort of
sea creature waiting to
be discovered. She can sing
quite well and has done a little acting.

Throwing a Fit!

Tentacle Lance
wants a chance
at the annual Octo-Dance,
but he's running behind
'cause he just cannot find
the appropriate
pair of pants!

But they're
Vertical.

Octomop

When Octavia Octopus went on vacation,
she forgot her eye glasses...
oh rot!
This caused quite a complication
when she fell madly in love with...
a mop!
(but they decided to go ahead
and give it a shot).

Seriously?

Dipping the Night Away

Time to bring out

all the sauce!

Now move around

just like a boss!

Honey mustard

and Sriracha!

Buttermilk ranch?

Okay, I gotchya!

Plain ol' kethcup?

Not to worry!

Here comes the garlic,

it's a dippin' flurry!

Lime pickle and cilantro,

barbecue so hearty,

all are welcome here!

It's a Spicy Chicken Nugget

Dance Party!!!

Pachydermatology

Everyone should know
(at least one would think)
it's foolish to give an elephant
a bath in the sink.

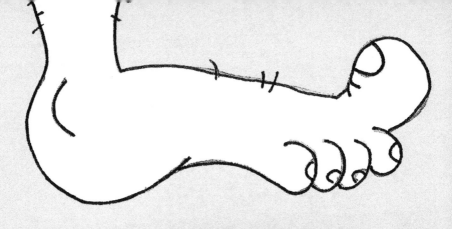

CHAPTER 6
Cheese, Feet, Fairy Tales & Other Stinky Things

Pooetry

It's been a while
since I wrote a poem
about doody or poo,
so I thought
that I had better
squeeze one out for you!

Ta-doo!

Always Be Prepared

One dark
and stormy night,
the mummy ran out
of toilet tissue!
It gave him
such a fright!
Okay... it really wasn't
that big of an issue.

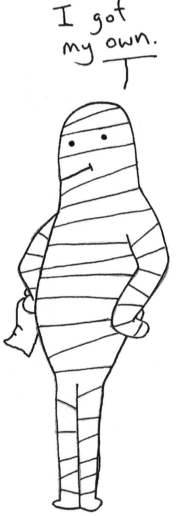

Foot Storm

I don't like feet.

They are gross, to say the most,

and they stink like rotten meat.

I don't like feet.

They get so smelly, upset my belly,

they can take a back seat.

I don't like feet.

Open toed shoes, give me the blues,

return 'em, here's the receipt.

I don't like feet.

Covered in germs, wiggle like worms,

even when they are petite.

I don't like feet.

Oozing with hair, fungus everywhere,

jagged nails rip the bed sheet.

I don't like feet.

Bumpy bunions, reek of onions,

I wish that they were obsolete....

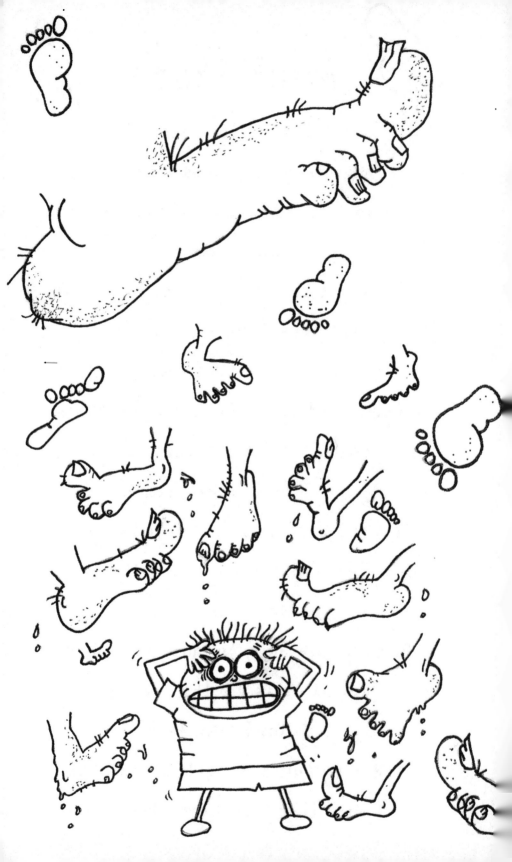

... I don't like feet.

Full of knobs and gooey globs,

yellow pus they do excrete.

I don't like feet.

Hang nails, corns and scales,

my disgust is complete

I don't like feet.

I do insist, if you're a podiatrist,

you must be crazy from the heat.

I don't like feet.

Icky, sticky, prickly, tickly,

day old, stale, gray and sickly feet!!!

I do not like feet!

Hey... wait a beat...

What's that odor? It's getting closer...

Okay, wait. This is just great.

It's a stampede of feet.

RETREAT!!!!!!!!!!!!!

Through the Looking Dude

Mirror, mirror on the wall,
Who's the fairest of them all?

Over the seven
sparkling falls,
beyond the
seventh wall,
in the dwelling
of the
seven dwarfs,
lives
SNOW WHITE...
FAIREST OF
THEM ALL!!!

I'm Nacho Enemy

Grab some tortilla chips!
Melt all of that cheese!
Add those jalapeno peppers!
Just as many as you please!
So, we've had a disagreement,
well, this will make amends
'cause everybody loves
eating NACHOS with their friends!

Look Out Below!

Cap'n Hook was troubled
by an itch upon his butt.
So, he went to scratch it.
Now, you might say, "so what?"
But here is the problem,
just between you and me,
he used the wrong "hand"
now it's a full moon at sea!

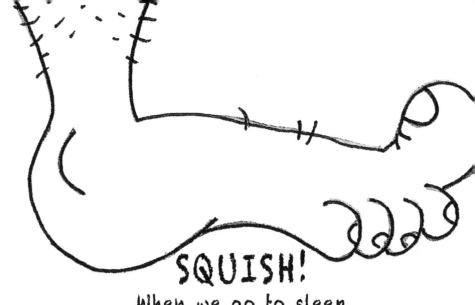

SQUISH!

When we go to sleep
and turn in for the night,
we tell one another,
"Don't let the bed bugs bite."
When the bed bugs go to sleep,
I wonder what they do,
maybe say to each other,
"Don't let the humans squash you!"

Bad Hair Day

When Rapunzel, Rapunzel
finally let down her hair,
it swallowed up the prince
and the whole town over there!

SAY CHEESE!

Cheesy Charles
liked to eat cheese.
May I have some more, sir?
He'd say "pretty please."
Pepper Jack and Brie,
Ricotta, chunk o' Cheddar,
Cheesy spread on cheesy bread?
Well, now that's even better!
There on the counter...
some sliced up Provolone!
It won't last long,
Charlie can't leave it alone!
Hey! Who went and ordered
that cheesy quesadilla?
Charlie just wants to say,
"That was a really good idea!"
Manchego and fine Feta,
how 'bout Mozzarella?
Uh, Charlie ate it all.
Well, he is a growing fella!

Nacho cheese flavored chips,
chile con algunos queso.
Would you like some, Charlie?
Well, I guess if you say so!
Cheese that is blue
and even Gorgonzola.
Cheese from a cottage?
Yeah, that's the rock-n-rolla!
Colby and crazy curds
Roquefort and Havarti
Cinnamon cream cheese?
Hey, now it's a party!
Charlie went to Tibet
to visit the Buddha.
The only question he had,
"Do you have any Gouda?"
So, it only kind of rhymes,
Charlie don't care about that,
so long as he's got
a big wheel of Monty Jack.

Always stuffing cheese into his mouth,
Muenster, Limburger,
all that Swiss...
Now when Charlie sees his wife,
he wonders why
she won't give him a kiss!

Gross.

That's too
much cheese.

The Toad Prince

The princess kissed a frog,
then felt just like a fool.
The frog turned into a prince
who turned out to be a tool.

Deli-ca-toe-ssen

Sandy the sand witch
grows teeth in her feet.
So, when she eats a sandwich,
all the toppings and the meat
that she finds and she fixes
get caught behind and betwixtes
her ten digits below,
and now she must floss
between each
and every
toe!

yum.

FLOSS

Free Thinker, Free Stinker

After seeing
a motivational speaker,
Sir Jonathan Whiskers MacSocks
decided to become
an inspirational seeker
by thinking outside of the box!

I'm my own cat.

CHAPTER 7
Zombies, Vampires, Witches... Wait a minute... Is it Halloween?

Arms Race

The zombies decided
to have an arms race,
from a spot over there
to some other place.
So, they all lined up
by the broken down house.
Then the zombie called Sid
put his foot in his mouth.
He grumbled and smiled,
"This arms race is mine!"
Sid mocked all the others,
giving them no piece of mind.
Next to Sid wobbled Sarah.
He said she was weak,
but Sarah just smiled
and kept her tongue in her cheek.

The zombie race started!
The whistle went "tweet!"
Sid immediately tripped
over his own two left feet!
Sarah hobbled along!
Sid continued to stumble!
Soon it was clear
that he would be humbled.

Sarah won the arms race
hand over fist.
When Sid staggered over,
what happened was this:
Sarah the zombie
told the zombie named Sid
to eat his heart out.
So, that's just what he did!

(It didn't taste too bad,
but it could've used a little salt).

Fangs of Fashion

Who is this dude
coming out of his mansion?
Looking so smooth,
the peak of all fashion!
Where did he get
that super sweet cloak?
Look at that collar,
it sure ain't no joke!
Covered all over
with plumb-crazy design,
He baffles the senses
and boggles the mind!
Squiggles and wiggles,
circles, triangles!
A geometrical puzzle
only he can untangle!

When the sun produces
a bit too much light,
he wraps himself up,
now this cat's outta sight!
You might catch a glimpse,
if you have any luck.
So, prepare for the awe
with which you will be struck!
The splendor might hit you
like an 18-wheel Mack truck!
He's the coolest of cool!
The squeakiest duck!
On top of his game!
He ain't no shmuck!
But don't dare dis his threads
or all your blood he will suck!!!
For he is...

...THE PAISLEY PRINCE OF DARKNESS!!!

(But his friends call him Chuck).

Divergent Detergent

Three Weird Sisters
cooking in a cave.
Bugs and blisters
coming from the grave.
Blue fires burn
and cauldrons bubble.
Live and learn
and toil and trouble.
Toe of frog
and eye of newt.
Tongue of dog
and rutabaga root.
Surf and tide
and rubbing alcohol.
Pinch of peroxide,
but that's not all...

A downy dash of dial,
a dove's fine feather.
Gain zest and style
with imperial leather.
Head and shoulders
give it glamour.
Make it bolder
with an arm and a hammer.
Dawn of joy,
cascading sunlight.
A little lifebuoy
and old, old spice.
It's almost done,
just one more thing.
Hot lava bubbling up
from an Irish Spring!
As the cat mews,
it's magic in motion.
Sputters & spews,
their life long potion!

But what will it do?
Put an end to all hope?
Is the whole world through???
Nope...
... they just made a bar of soap.

Gone Shopping

Who is that
ringing at the front door?
If it's the grim reaper,
kindly tell him
I went to the store.

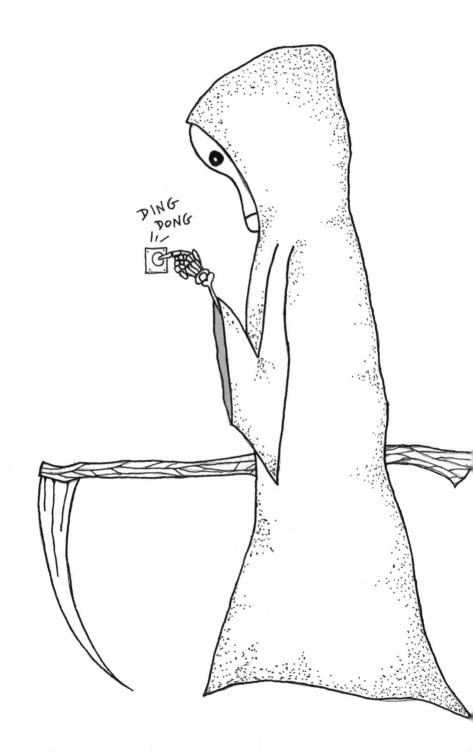

Wind Beneath My Wish

The Headless Horseman's homies
busted out a bash with birthday cake.
No invitation for Brom Bonesie,
things were great for goodness' sake!
But then arose a situation,
no one quite knew how to handle,
when it came time to make some wishin'
he could not put out the candles!

Blow
'em out.

Ummm...

The Scarlet-Toothed Pumpernickel

The butter's disappeared!

The jelly can't be found!

The marmalade's gone missing!

The cinnamon's not around!

There can only be one reason,

the condiments

went underground!

The vicious, delicious,

not so nutritious

Vampire Toast...

has come back

to town!

Finger Food

A Zom-B-Q
is quite different from a Bar-B-Q.
If you request a ham-burger
on gluten-free bread,
you'll most likely get
a HAND-burger
(on whole-wheat bun)
instead.

Bring It!

I got two shoes on my feet,
so I'm gonna walk all day.
Getting ready to meet
whatever comes my way.
I can handle anything
no matter if it's frightening.
Whatever life may bring,
I'll find it so enlightening.
Here I go, I'm running,
This world is my oyster.
Hurricanes are coming?
Bah! Just a little moisture!
Nothing will hold me back.
There's nothing I won't face.
An alien Martian attack?
I'll send 'em back to outer space!
Dragons breathing fire?
Water puts out any match.
Fences of barbed wire?
A Band-Aid fixes that scratch!

Zombies hoping to munch
upon my cerebral section?
Gobble it up for lunch?
I'll give them indigestion!
Creatures of the night?
Goblins and twelve Ghouls?
Ghosts who mean to fright?
They're all a bunch of fools!
I ain't afraid of nothing.
I'll take whatever as it comes.
I ain't never bluffing.
Give me trouble in tens & fives & ones!
Stepping outside my door,
gonna take this world for a ride...
Wait a minute...
Is that a spider on the floor???
Okay...
I'm going back inside.

163.

Shadow of a Doubt

Shadow, shadow
Following me
Could you be mine?
I guess you could be.
Shadow, shadow
Do you belong to me?
I have my doubts,
Not sure I wanna find out.
Shadow, shadow
Let's look at the facts,
You could be mine
but alas...
I'm not
carrying an axe!

The Gravedigger's Daughter

The gravedigger's daughter
cried such tears of dew.
Her father sat her down,
"My dear, what troubles you?"
The gravedigger's daughter
said, "I am so powerful blue,
'cause you bury everybody,
but when the time comes,
who will bury you?"
The gravedigger smiled, he
said, "Here is a clue,
this shovel in my hand,
it is so grand,
and daughter, I plan
on giving it to you."

The House Over There

You must beware
of the house over there.
Born from a nightmare
was the house over there.
Do not stare
at the house over there.
Go anywhere
except the house over there.
Best say a prayer
if you're going to the house over there.
Be sure you've paid your healthcare
before going to the house over there.
Cover yourself in honey and visit a bear
instead of going to the house over there.
Hang out with a guy named Pierre.
Read a book by Voltaire.
Sit in a broken chair.
Wash your brother's underwear.
But whatever you do, don't you dare
go anywhere near
the house over there!!!

"Why must we stay clear
of the house over there?"
Oh... I'm just saying things,
I really don't care.

Are You Ready to Rock?

This creature of the night

does not have a lot of cares.

He'll learn to rock 'n' roll

if it takes a hundred years.

But he might need a couple more,

at least that's how it's seemin'

'cause his nickname on the street

is currently the "Tone Deaf Demon."

But it's all cool and all good

for this rocker called Count Dracula.

For in another century or two,

he's gonna be spec-TACULA!

Waist No Words

The monsters rolled around,

wreaking havoc up and down.

Folks were scared

and no one dared

to chase them out of town.

Then came little Mrs. Pipps,

few words flowing from her lips,

but tired of these fools,

she stopped all of the ghouls,

by simply putting

her hands

upon her

hips.

Her stern demeanor
Frightens me.

Counting the Days

Little Mindy Mason May
thinks it's just the worst,
her fiendish friends refuse to play
until October Thirty-First.
The Wolfman and ol' Drac,
Mummy and Frankenstein,
zany zombie Zack,
and those skulls without a spine.
They lock and
latch the door,
making Mindy
want to scream,
the whole year
is such a bore,
why can't
every day
be HALLOWEEN!?!?

Barking Up
the Wrong Lily Pad

This is a dog.

Dressed as a Frog.

For Halloween.

Woof.

Sweet & Sour Dreams

It's time to go to bed.

No nightmares in your head...

Except for that one

with the pale vampire.

Or the wild werewolf

that makes you perspire.

And remember the one

where you're trying to swim,

but you keep on seeing

that giant shark fin!

And then there's the one,

you hate it the most,

staring at you all night

is a torn up old ghost!

And this one is great,

you can't help the feeling

that spiders are dangling

from every inch of the ceiling!

And now for a classic
that drives you insane!
Zombies are biting
and eating your brain!
And this one's the best,
the worst of them all.
You slide off a cliff
and just fall and fall and fall,
forever into darkness unseen,
and no one can hear your screams.
Well...
sweet dreams.
Happy Halloween!
(or any day in between)

CHAPTER 8

Needles, Threads
& Loose Ends
or
The Island of
Misfit Poems

Rhyme
of the Silly Mariner

A life at sea,
that is for me.
Or so says the old quote.
And I do decree,
I'd like it to be,
but I can't fit inside of my boat!

Sew What?

Ain't got no fingers
or likewise toes,
don't see any ears,
or any kind of nose,
got rid of my hair,
along with the rest,
traded everything in
for this super sweet vest.
Why would I do that?
Seems silly... say what?
Sorry, I can't answer,
I done
sewn my mouth shut!

186.

Threadbare

I found a hair
stickin' out my forehead.
I pulled that hair
as if it were a thread.
Now that hair
has got me cursin'
'cause
pullin'
that
hair
un
raveled
my
whole
darn
person!

It's Around Here Somewhere...

This really ain't no joke.
I own an invisible cloak.
I could throw it on and hide,
accomplish anything that I tried,
eat all the pasta fettucine,
not a single soul would see me,
go from Cairo to Carrizozo
and you would never know, bro,
secretly play dad's synthesizer,
he would never be the wiser,
become an enlightened despot,
and no one would ever guess it,
chill with that wee fella and his ring,
do just about any darned old thing.
I would be the most powerful of blokes
with my sweet, wonderful, invisible cloak,
rule every city, every village, every town!
If I could just remember...

... where the heck I set it down!

On a One Horse Broken Sleigh

I put on my hat and scarf
to go for a sleigh ride.
But I showed up late,
so I was left behind.
By the look of things,
I think that worked out fine.
Hey! Hello, down there!
Havin' a good time?

The Adventures of The Adventures!

There's a new group of heroes
who recently moved to town.
Lookin' to fight some bad guys,
they're ready to throw down.
They call themselves "The Adventures"
For real and they ain't fakin'...
They would've used a different name,
but all the good ones had been taken.
This is who these heroes are
just in case you might see them around...
Tired Tim, Bell Head, Blob Cat, Spicy Chicken
and some guy who kinda looks like a clown.

Seriously?

Yep.

Stopping crime and saving lives,
they're ready to do a bunch!
But it's almost noon o' clock,
so first things first,
time for an adventure
with some lunch!

THE BIG SCOOP

I got a giant ice cream cone
It's so much bigger than me!
How am I s'posed to eat it?
This certainly cannot be!
I bet I'll get real sick
'cause it ain't sugar-free
& gain so many pounds
I would say at least
seventy-three!
Then regret will
take over, and
I'll be so
unhappy
If I eat
this ice
cream
cone
That's so much bigger than me.

I could always share it.
Oh! I think I might!
That sounds pretty good.
Would you like a bite?

Adeline's Idea

Adeline,
that funny friend of mine,
had a brain made out of Jello.
She thought it'd be fine
to buy a porcupine
and use it for her pillow!

HANG IN THERE!
(A Little Affirmation)

Your life
might seem cursed
with heartaches,
bad breaks
and
mistakes!
But it could
always be worse,
at least
you're not about
to be eaten
by a whole
bunch of
snakes!

Compromise

This is not
the hat
that I wanted
to wear...
...but I
could not
find
the other
one...
anywhere.

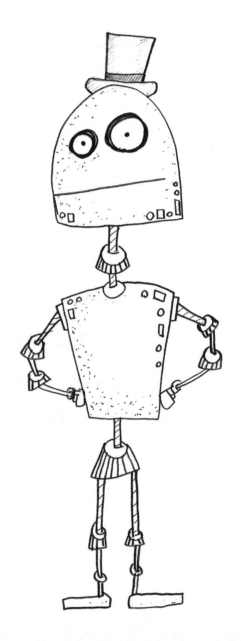

Cheeky Shoulder

When one is
feeling
sad and weak,
nothing's quite so
healing
as a shoulder
for the cheek.

What's the Deal?

I have written no poem or story
for this funny, little guy,
so he keeps calling for me,
demanding to know why.
Now all I can think to say,
when he counters with that look,
is, "I've run out of ideas today,
but I'll fit you in the next book!"

What am I?
Chopped liver?

INDEX

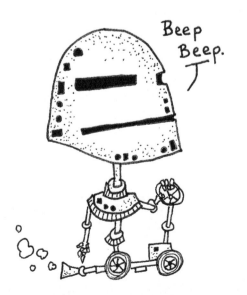

Beep
Beep.

Ribbit
Ribbit.

And now a great, big
THANK YOU
to the
following folks!

Aaron Hendren, Aidan & Micah,
Alice Elizabeth Meaney, Allana Vigliotti,
Allison "Monkey" Andrade, Andi Januskiewicz,
Andrew J. Kim, Andy Elliott, Ann Pennington,
Astrid Tuttle Winegar, Blue, Bones,
Brian Bhandey, Bryan H. Quackenbush,
Callum Orr, Chelsea & Thomas McKeen
Chris & Sarah Suski, Christina,
Christina Cavaleri, Cindy Maples, Cody Jae,
Craig A. Butler, D. Marie,
Daniel & Calista Lopez, David Valdez, Dawn,
Denise Schulz, Doctor Daniel, Doug Montoya,
Ed Wallander, Elizabeth Quintero-Dawson,
Elliot Jackson, Emily Newkirk,
Emma & Elanor Wenrich, Erin "Erni" Wolf,
Finn Ray, FoolSinc, Gavin & Ian White,
George Bach, George Simon a.k.a. "UG",
Grace & Garrett Uithoven, Henry Coffman, J.,
Jason & Starla Barrett, Jesse, Joan & Andrew,
Julie Ann Glaz-Bopp, Khloe Marie Peterson,
LCMH, Lee Francis IV, Leonard & Jane Witter,
Linus Loscher, Lisa McCoy, Lisa Sustaita,

Lucas Kottke, Mae Diseth, Maggie S,
Marilyn Howard, Mark & Amanda, Mary Danish,
Matthew Urbaniak & Charlotte Urbaniak
Mia, Mia & Sebastian Bernstein,
Mike "Superman" Wilson, Moniza Kanani,
MOOTS!,
Morgan, Tiffany, Shayla, Ian & Keira,
Nadia Heller, Nathan Erickson,
Norwitz Family, Nova C, Oliver Karas-Frale,
Olivia DeLoach,
Phil & Jenn, Rachel Martin,
Ray & Beth Welt, Riley Clemence, Rob Buco,
Rob Fowler, Rory & Liam Bootsma,
Ryan Denmark, Ryan Moore,
Sugar Lagoon - Sami Denny, Sevrina,
Scott & Baby Gibson,
Sophie Nicole Unsworth, Stephanie Chambers,
Stephanie Shelton, Tammie Classen,
Terri The Terrible, The Donuts,
Tina Benjamin, Virginia Ludvik,
Wil Bartleman, Winston Kou

More Books by Jason L. Witter

Collections of
poems & illustrations:

"The Tiniest Vampire"
(and other silly things)

"Monsters Eating Ice Cream"
(and other silly things)

CLASSICS (kind of)
Silly new adaptations of cool old stories

Bram Stoker's "Dracula"

Edgar Allan Poe's "The Raven"

Herman Melville's "Moby Dick"

Homer's "The Odyssey"

William Shakespeare's "Hamlet"

"The Tiniest Vampire"
(a coloring adventure)

All books available on Amazon.com

Contact Jason at witterworks1@gmail.com

Made in the USA
Columbia, SC
23 June 2018